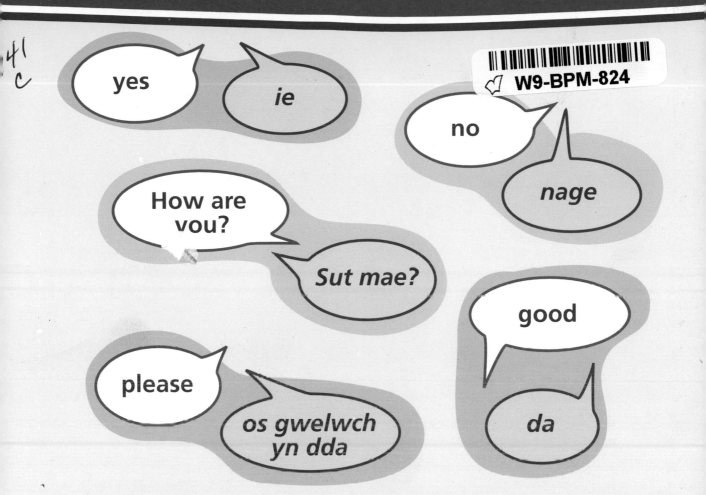

English words that come from Welsh

cairn   coracle   corgi   flannel

Cockney rhyming slang

apples and pairs	stairs	dog and bone	phone
bacon and eggs	legs	frog and toad	road
bag of fruit	suit	Noah's Ark	shark
bangers and mash	cash	Pat Malone	alone
bricks and mortar	daughter	plates of meat	feet
butcher's hook	look	porky pies	lies
dead horse	tomato sauce	trouble and strife	wife

Welcome to the United Kingdom

the

Meredith Costain Paul Collins

This edition first published in 2002 in the United States of America by Chelsea House Publishers, a subsidiary of Haights Cross Communications

Chelsea House Publishers
1974 Sproul Road, Suite 400
Broomall, PA 19008–0914

The Chelsea House world wide web address is www.chelseahouse.com

Library of Congress Cataloging-in-Publication Data Applied for.
ISBN 0-7910-6544-8

First published in 2000 by
Macmillan Education Australia Pty Ltd
627 Chapel Street, South Yarra, Australia, 3141

Copyright © Meredith Costain and Paul Collins 2000

Edited by Miriana Dasovic
Text design and page layout by Goanna Graphics (Vic) Pty Ltd
Cover design by Goanna Graphics (Vic) Pty Ltd
Maps by Stephen Pascoe
Illustrations by Vaughan Duck
Printed in Hong Kong

Acknowledgements
The author and the publisher are grateful to the following for permission to reproduce copyright material:

Cover photograph: A Scottish piper, © Malvine Roberth.

AUSCAPE, p. 21 (bottom) © Keith Ringland-OSF; Anne Connelly pp. 18 (left), 30; Angela Costain pp. 6, 30; Michelle Gilliland pp. 5, 7, 8; Blaine Harrington pp. 12 (right), 18 (right), 20, 21 (top), 23, 25 (top), 29; Lonely Planet Images, p. 14 © Bethune Carmichael, pp. 11, 15 (top) © Juliet Coombe, p. 12 (left) © Doug McKinlay, pp. 24, 25 (bottom) © Chris Mellor, p. 13 © Guy Moberly, p. 9 © David Wall; Malvine Roberth pp. 10, 15 (bottom), 19, 22, 26–8, 30.

While every care has been taken to trace and acknowledge copyright the publishers tender their apologies for any accidental infringement where copyright has proved untraceable.

Contents

Capital city
Major cities
Other cities

N

Dornie
Loch Ness
Ben Nevis Spey River
Dee River
Grampian Highlands
Firth of Forth
Glasgow • Edinburgh
SCOTLAND
NORTHUMBERLAND
North Sea
NORTHERN IRELAND
Loch Neagh
• Belfast
Bann River
Lake District
Pennines
REPUBLIC OF IRELAND
LANCASHIRE
• Leeds
Mersey River
• Manchester
Liverpool
• Sheffield
CHESHIRE
Bakewell
Mt Snowdon
STAFFORDSHIRE
• Birmingham
Ouse River
• Stratford-upon-Avon
WALES
Severn River
Thames River
• Grendon Underwood
NETHERLANDS
Cardiff
Bath
Avebury
London
Cheddar
WILTSHIRE
BELGIUM
• Stonehenge
SOMERSET
DORSET
Southampton
CORNWALL
English Channel
FRANCE

Welcome to the United Kingdom!

Hi! My name is Holly and I come from Grendon Underwood, in Buckinghamshire, England.

England is one of the countries that make up the United Kingdom. The other countries are Scotland, Wales and Northern Ireland. Our nation is often referred to as Britain, and our people are often called British. The United Kingdom covers only a small area, but it has a large population. We are separated from the mainland of western Europe by the English Channel. Our nearest neighbors to the east are France, Belgium and the Netherlands. The Republic of Ireland is to the west.

The United Kingdom has a long history. Over the centuries, people from many different nations and cultures have settled in our country. The most recent arrivals have come from the Caribbean and Africa, and from south-Asian countries such as India, Pakistan and Bangladesh.

Our flag features the crosses of St. George, St. Andrew and St. Patrick. They are the patron saints of England, Scotland and Ireland. Our flag's real name is the Union Flag, but many people call it the Union Jack. English is our official language, but people in some regions still speak their traditional languages. Some people speak Welsh in Wales, Gaelic in Scotland, and Irish Gaelic in Northern Ireland.

Family life

Grendon Underwood is a quiet village in Buckinghamshire, northwest of London. There are some lovely old houses in our village. One of them is called 'Shakespeare House', because people say Shakespeare once stayed here on his way to London. There is also a church, a school, a village shop and a post office.

My father, Stewart, is a marketing and sales director for a beer company. My mother, Michelle, is studying part-time at college. I have an older brother, Daniel, who plays rugby for his school. Grandma and Grandad live nearby. I often take their dog Dougal for a walk. He loves it when I brush his coat.

*This is our house. It is more than 300 years old. The doorframes are all quite low, because people were much shorter when it was built! My bedroom is upstairs, under the **thatched roof**. The window looks out to the front street.*

My family on a visit to Dunster Castle in Somerset. We travel to many different places on the weekends.

My class went on a school trip to a wildlife park. I liked the long-eared rabbits best. I used to have two pet rabbits, but they escaped.

On weekends I play with my next-door neighbor, Siobhan. We play computer games, listen to music and make up dance routines. My favorite bands are Ricky Martin, B*Witched, Steps and Boyzone. Sometimes Siobhan sleeps over. We put on make-up, paint our fingernails and tell each other lots of secrets. If the weather is good, we play tennis or jump on the trampoline.

School

British children start school when they are five. Many first go to kindergarten or nursery school for a few years. After two years in infants' school, children move on to junior school until they are 11 or 12. After junior school, students complete their secondary education at a comprehensive (general), grammar (academic) or secondary modern (technical) school. Students need to pass an exam called the '11 plus' to be accepted into a grammar school.

My school day starts at 8:50 a.m. and finishes at 3:45 p.m. After school, we can stay at our 'Tea Club' until 6:00 p.m. My subjects include maths, English, French, Latin, science, history, sport, art and Scripture. My favorite subject is history. I always wanted to be a vet. Now that I have seen animal operations on TV, I am not so sure!

Our school play last year was Charlie and the Chocolate Factory. *I played an Oompa Loompa. That's me in the front row, second from the left.*

Sports and leisure

British people love sports. When we are not playing sports ourselves, we love watching it from a stadium or on TV. Many of the sports played around the world first started in the United Kingdom. They include soccer, which we call football, rugby, cricket, tennis and golf.

Our world-class stadiums and playing fields are famous for their sporting events. There is tennis at Wimbledon, football at Wembley, cricket at Lord's, rugby union at Cardiff Arms Park and golf at St. Andrews.

The Highland Games are held in Scotland each year. People compete in events such as highland dancing, bagpipe playing, 'throwing the hammer' and 'tossing the caber'. Gaelic football, handball, **hurling**, rounders and *camogie* (women's hurling) are played at the Gaelic Games in Northern Ireland.

The British also spend a lot of time watching television and videos, and listening to music on the radio. Two of our popular soap operas are 'Coronation Street' and 'EastEnders'. Other popular leisure activities include fishing, walking, mountain-climbing, snooker and going to aerobics classes.

A cricket match at Warkworth Castle in Northumberland, England. Cricket was first played in southeast England in the 1700s.

British culture

We have a rich cultural history in the United Kingdom. London is one of the leading centers for the arts. Our theaters, opera houses and ballet companies are world class. The Edinburgh International Festival is the largest arts festival in the world.

Our famous literature includes Chaucer's *Canterbury Tales*, the novels of Charles Dickens and Jane Austen, the plays of William Shakespeare and Tom Stoppard, and the poems of Dylan Thomas and Seamus Heaney.

We are also famous for our sense of humor. Some of our funniest comedians include John Cleese, Peter Sellers and Charlie Chaplin. Comedies such as 'The Goon Show', 'Monty Python's Flying Circus', 'Fawlty Towers' and 'Absolutely Fabulous' are known throughout the world.

We have many different styles of music, ranging from classical and jazz to world and folk music. In the 1960s, rock'n'roll bands such as the Beatles, The Who and the Rolling Stones took the world by storm. These days, bands such as Blur, Oasis and the Spice Girls top the charts.

*A Scottish piper wearing a **tartan** kilt and **sporran**. Each Scottish clan, or family, has its own tartan pattern.*

*A festival is held each year in Stratford-upon-Avon to celebrate the works of our greatest **playwright**, William Shakespeare. People dress up as characters from his many plays.*

Art galleries such as the National Gallery and the Tate Gallery in London, and the Scottish National Portrait Gallery in Edinburgh, contain many fine examples of British art. Our famous artists include J.M.W. Turner, John Constable, and the sculptor Henry Moore.

Morris dancing has been performed in English country villages for centuries. The male dancers wear straw hats, ribbons, and jingling bells on their knees.

Festivals and religion

Most people in the United Kingdom are Christian. There are many Christian groups, including Anglicans, Roman Catholics, Presbyterians, Methodists and Baptists. A smaller number of people follow the Muslim, Hindu, Jewish or Sikh religions.

Every June, the Queen's birthday is celebrated with a ceremony known as 'Trooping the Color'.

Many towns and villages celebrate local traditions each year. They hold colorful parades and carnivals. The Welsh celebrate their national day by wearing daffodils and leeks, a type of onion. In Northern Ireland, three-leaved plants called shamrocks are worn on St Patrick's Day.

Westminster Abbey. Our kings and queens have been crowned here for the past 900 years.

A colorful carnival is held every year in Notting Hill, London.

There are many traditions in the United Kingdom for celebrating the new year. In Scotland and northern England, the '**first footer**' brings coal, bread, whisky and good luck to people's homes. In Wales, the back door is opened at the first stroke of midnight to release the Old Year. It is then locked to 'keep the luck in' until the last stroke, when the New Year is let in at the front door.

On Halloween, children roam the streets dressed as ghosts and witches. They carry candles made from pumpkins. Guy Fawkes Night is named after the man who tried to blow up the Houses of Parliament in 1605. People let off fireworks, light bonfires and burn stuffed figures of Guy Fawkes.

British festivals and holidays

New Year's Day	January 1
Burns' Night (Scotland)	January 25
St. David's Day (Wales)	March 1
St. Patrick's Day (Northern Ireland)	March 17
St. George's Day (England)	April 23
May Day	beginning of May
Queen's Birthday	June
Halloween	October 31
Guy Fawkes Night	November 5
Christmas	December 25

Food and shopping

Much of our food is named after the area from which it came. Cheeses such as Cheshire, Lancashire and Cheddar come from villages or counties with those names. Cornwall, in southern England, is famous for its Cornish pasties. Other dishes that are named after places are Lancashire hotpot, Welsh rarebit, Bath buns and Bakewell tarts. HP sauce was created by the chef at the Houses of Parliament!

Haggis and neeps (turnips) is Scotland's national dish. Haggis is made by stuffing a sheep's stomach with lamb's offal, which is the lungs, liver and heart. The offal is mixed with a type of fat called suet, and with onions, herbs and spices. It is then cooked.

A chicken stall at Portobello Road Market in Kensington, London. The market sells everything from jewelry and antiques, to flowers and fruit.

Harrods, in the West End of London, is one of our most famous shops. Members of the Royal Family often shop here, but only after hours!

The most popular meal in Britain is fish and chips. We also enjoy 'bangers and mash', which are sausages with mashed potatoes, and roast beef with Yorkshire pudding and gravy. These days, our restaurants and fast-food shops offer food from all over the world. You can eat Indian, Italian, Greek, American and Chinese food here. My favorite foods are pasta, pizza, fruit and chocolate.

Make Welsh rarebit

This dish is pronounced Welsh 'rabbit', although you won't find any bunnies in this recipe!

Ask an adult to help you prepare this dish.

You will need:

- 100 grams (1/2 cup) cheddar cheese, grated
- 1 teaspoon mustard
- 2 tablespoons milk
- 2 slices bread
- butter or margarine
- a pinch of salt and pepper

What to do:

1 Mix together the grated cheese, mustard and milk to make the 'rarebit'.

2 Lightly grill or toast both sides of the bread.

3 Butter the toast, then spread it with the rarebit mixture.

4 Put the toast under the grill until the rarebit is bubbly and golden brown. Season with salt and pepper.

5 Cut the toast into two pieces. Enjoy!

Play conkers

In the autumn, we collect chestnuts to play 'conkers'. Some kids bake their conkers in the oven to harden them, even though this is cheating!

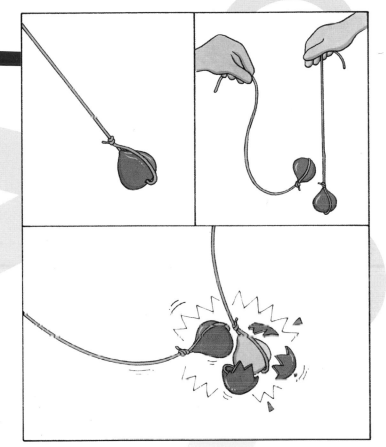

You will need:

- chestnuts
- a drill, or a hammer and nail
- lengths of string, about 40 cm (16 in) each

What to do

1 Ask an adult to help you drill a hole through the center of each chestnut.

2 Thread a piece of string through each hole. Tie a firm knot to keep it in place

Rules of play

1 The first player holds up their conker by the end of its string. The second player swings their conker at the first player's conker. The goal is to break the other player's conker.

2 If the conker does not break, the first player then swings at the second player's conker. The players keep taking turns at swinging until one of the conkers breaks.

3 The player whose conker does not break is the champion. They can now defend their title against other players.

Landscape and climate

The United Kingdom is made up of many different landscapes. We have rolling green fields, gentle hills, rocky mountains, deep lakes, **peaty marshes** and bleak **moors**.

The Pennines, a chain of limestone mountains, run down the middle of England like a spine. Our highest mountain is Ben Nevis, in the Grampian Highlands. Snowdon is the highest peak in Wales. It is part of Snowdonia, an area that is popular with climbers in the summer.

Rydal Water in the Lake District, northern England.

Eilean Donan Castle on the edge of Loch Duich, on the west coast of Scotland. The castle has appeared in films such as Bonnie Prince Charlie, Highlander *and the* James Bond movie, The World is Not Enough.

The land along the Dorset Coast in southern England has been eaten away by the sea.

Average temperatures		
	January	July
London	4°C/39°F	17°C/63°F
Cardiff	6°C/43°F	16°C/61°F
Edinburgh	3°C/37°F	15°C/59°F
Belfast	5°C/41°F	15°C/59°F

The Giant's Causeway, in Northern Ireland, looks like a set of stepping stones for a giant. Its six-sided rocks were formed by lava from a volcano. Over the centuries, ice has worn away the land in the Scottish highlands and in the Lake District to form deep valleys and long lakes. Lakes are known as 'lochs' in Scotland. Loch Ness is famous for its mythical monster!

Although our weather is often wet and cloudy, our climate is quite mild. Temperatures rarely rise above 32°C (90°F) or fall below −10°C (14°F). Our driest months are March to June, and our wettest are September to January. The highland areas of the west and north receive the most rain.

Plants and animals

Hundreds of years ago, most of Britain was covered with forests of oak, beech, pine and birch trees. Over time, the trees were cut down to provide timber for housing and land for farms and towns. The government is now encouraging people to protect existing woodlands, and to plant new trees when old ones are cut down. Hedges that form boundaries between fields, known as hedgerows, are also disappearing. Three-quarters of our native lowland animals and birds, and half of our butterfly species, breed in hedges.

Britain's national plants

England – rose

Scotland – thistle

Northern Ireland – shamrock

Wales – daffodil and leek

A carpet of wildflowers in a field in Wiltshire, southern England. Heather, gorse and bracken grow wild in the highland regions of Britain.

A lamb at Dornie, in the Scottish highlands. These days, most of Britain is covered with farmland.

A red squirrel runs along a trail in Scotland. Squirrels are also found in many London parks.

Foxes and badgers live in woodland areas. We have over 400 different types of birds, including robins, swans, and wrens, which are our smallest type of bird. The adder is our only poisonous snake. There are about 30 different types of freshwater fish, and seals live along our coast.

Cities and landmarks

Before the 1800s, most people lived in the country and worked on farms. London was our only large city. After the **Industrial Revolution** many people flocked to towns, looking for work in factories. Towns like Birmingham, Manchester, Glasgow and Belfast grew to become cities. London continued to grow too. These days, many jobs in the industrial towns of the north have been lost. Many people have moved south to London and other parts of southeast England to find work.

The Tower Bridge is one of London's most famous landmarks. It was built in 1894. The middle part is raised to let ocean-going ships pass underneath. An American oil company bought London Bridge, which is an older bridge further along the Thames River. The company thought it was buying the Tower Bridge! It had the London Bridge taken to pieces and rebuilt in Arizona.

Edinburgh Castle is built on an ancient volcanic rock which towers above the streets of the city. The castle has been used as a fort for over 2,000 years. Many Scottish kings and queens have lived here. Over the centuries, it has been captured and recaptured many times by the English.

The United Kingdom is full of interesting places to visit. You can choose from Roman ruins, stately homes, historic villages, crumbling castles and towering **cathedrals**. London's many famous landmarks include St. Paul's Cathedral, Piccadilly Circus and Buckingham Palace. The Tower of London is a large fortress containing many smaller towers. It was the scene of many beheadings. The skeletons of two young boys were found buried beneath the steps of the White Tower in the 1600s. They were believed to be the sons of King Edward IV, who were murdered in the Bloody Tower in 1483.

Big Ben, at the top of St. Stephen's Tower in the Houses of Parliament, London. Most people think the name refers to the clock, but Big Ben is actually the brass bell inside the tower.

23

Industry and agriculture

The United Kingdom has more natural resources of **fuel** than any other European country. There are large reserves of coal, oil and gas. We also use **nuclear power** stations, **wind turbines** and **solar panels** to produce electricity to power our country.

We are the fifth-largest trading nation in the world. We are also a major supplier of machinery, cars and trucks, and aerospace products such as space satellites and guided weapons. Six out of the eleven Formula 1 car makers are based here.

The United Kingdom is also the fifth-largest producer of chemicals, and the third-biggest exporter of medicines in the world. Our electronic products include computers, automatic cash dispensers and high-tech television sets. More than three-quarters of our people work in service industries such as banking, retail, catering and tourism.

The cooling towers of a power station in Staffordshire, England.

Highland cattle in Scotland.

Almost three-quarters of our land area is used for farming. Over half our farms stock dairy cattle, beef cattle or sheep. Our major crops are wheat, barley, oilseeds, sugar beet and potatoes. Most of these are grown in eastern and central southern England, and in eastern Scotland.

Fish are caught mainly in the North Sea, off the coasts of northeast England and eastern Scotland. Many fishing **trawlers** contain freezers, so they can stay at sea for a long time.

Modern machines are used to harvest crops. Before the Industrial Revolution, fields were worked by hand.

Transportation

There are many ways of travelling around the United Kingdom. The most popular is by road. Our first roads were built many centuries ago by the Romans. Today, more than 400,000 kilometers (248,560 miles) of roads crisscross the nation. Although our motorways make up only one percent of our road network, they carry 16 percent of its traffic. London's famous double-decker buses carry about four million passengers daily.

London is famous for its large black taxis.

London's Heathrow is one of the busiest international airports in the world. Over 50 million passengers pass through its gates each year. Our major airlines are British Airways, Britannia and Virgin Atlantic. We have over 80 important seaports. These include London, Forth, Southampton, Belfast and Liverpool.

Hovercraft 'float' above water or land on a cushion of air. They are much faster than ferries.

Our Eurostar trains are fast. They take less than three hours to deliver passengers from the international terminal at Waterloo, in London, to the center of Paris. The Channel Tunnel was built under the English Channel. It connects our rail network with the European mainland. Fast inter-city trains whiz passengers around the country. Local 'stopping' trains take people to smaller towns and villages. Both London and Glasgow have an underground rail service.

A modern London bus on its way to Heathrow.

History and government

Our history is a story of invasion and settlement. People have been living in this country since prehistoric times. They left behind impressive monuments, such as Stonehenge on Salisbury Plain and the stone circle at Avebury. A group of people called Celts first settled on the mainland over 2,500 years ago. Welsh, a Celtic language, is still spoken in Wales today.

The Romans invaded Britain in AD 43 and stayed for 300 years. They were brilliant organizers who built waterways, roads, cities and towns. The Angles, Saxons and Jutes were Germanic peoples who began raiding and settling Britain around AD 200. Scots from Ireland began to settle the northern part of Britain, now known as Scotland, around AD 500. The Vikings arrived from Scandinavia 200 years later. The last invaders were the Normans. They came in 1066.

The next 1,000 years produced many historic events. The Magna Carta, signed by King John in 1215, brought new freedoms to the people of Britain. Civil war broke out in 1642. England united with Wales and Scotland to form Great Britain.

*Stonehenge is our most famous prehistoric monument. Some people think it was built by **Druids** 5,000 years ago, as a place to worship the sun.*

From the 1600s through to the 1800s, Britain expanded its empire overseas. The Industrial Revolution in the late 1700s changed people's lives forever. The 20th century brought two world wars. Many British cities were bombed, and city children were sent away to safety in the country.

Today the United Kingdom is part of the **European Union**. We have a democratic system of government. This means that we are able to choose who runs the country. Our parliament has three sections. They are the **monarchy**, the **House of Commons** and the **House of Lords**. In 1999, Scotland and Wales set up their own parliaments. This gave them more control over their own affairs.

Hadrian's Wall was built by the Romans in AD 122 to keep the fearsome Scottish tribes out of Britain.

Fact file

Official name United Kingdom of Great Britain and Northern Ireland		**Population** 59,000,000	**Land area** 242,820 square kilometers (94,700 square miles)
Government parliamentary democracy	**Languages** English, Welsh, Gaelic		**Religions** Mainly Christianity, but also Islam, Sikhism, Hinduism, Judaism
Currency Pound sterling (£) £1 = 100 pence		**Capital city** London	**Major cities** Birmingham, Glasgow, Leeds, Sheffield, Liverpool, Edinburgh, Cardiff, Belfast, Manchester
		Climate variable, but generally mild and cloudy	
Major rivers Thames, Severn, Spey, Dee, Ouse, Bann, Mersey	**Largest lake** Lough Neagh in Northern Ireland 396 square kilometers (154 square miles)		**Highest mountain** Ben Nevis, Scotland 1,343 meters (4,406 feet)
Main farm products barley, wheat, vegetables, oilseed, cattle, sheep, poultry, fish	**Main industries** steel, machinery, cars, shipbuilding, aircraft, chemicals, coal, paper, food processing		**Natural resources** oil, coal, natural gas, tin, limestone, iron ore, salt, clay

Glossary

cathedrals	large churches with magnificent architecture
Druids	Celtic priests who lived in Britain before the arrival of Christianity. They were excellent astronomers
European Union	a group of European countries with both economic and political ties
first footer	the first person to enter the house after midnight in the new year
fuel	a natural material that is burned to produce energy
House of Commons	the elected members of Parliament, whose main purpose is to make laws and discuss political issues
House of Lords	90 members of Parliament who are not elected but who inherited their positions from family members. Their main purpose is to examine and review laws made by the House of Commons
hurling	a Gaelic sport, like a cross between hockey and football
Industrial Revolution	a time at the end of the 1700s, when people moved to the cities to work in factories rather than farming the land
monarchy	the king or queen
moors	areas of open land, often covered with a shrub known as heath
nuclear power	energy that is obtained by splitting the atom rather than by burning fuel
peaty marsh	dense, rich soil that is made of rotting grass (peat) and is found in low, swampy land (marshes). Peat can be cut out of the ground and used as fuel
playwright	a writer of plays
solar panels	panels that collect energy from the sun
sporran	a goatskin pouch worn over the front of a kilt
tartan	a checked woollen cloth used to make kilts
thatched roof	a roof made from straw
trawlers	boats that drag nets behind them to catch fish
wind turbines	modern types of windmill used to produce electricity

Index